BE A PLUMBER

Published in the United States of America by Cherry Lake Publishing
Ann Arbor, Michigan
www.cherrylakepublishing.com

Reading Adviser: Marla Conn, MS, Ed., Literacy specialist, Read-Ability, Inc.

Photo Credits: Cover and pages 1 and 20, ©Andrey_Popov/Shutterstock; page 5, ©IanRedding/Shutterstock; page 6, ©asadykov/Shutterstock; page 8, ©wong yu liang/Shutterstock; page 10, ©Prasit Rodphan/Shutterstock; page 12, ©goodluz/Shutterstock; page 14, ©ALPA PROD/Shutterstock; page 16, ©Rawpixel.com/Shutterstock; page 19, ©Smit/Shutterstock; pages 22 and 26, ©Dragon Images/Shutterstock; pages 25 and 28, ©Monkey Business Images/Shutterstock

Library of Congress Cataloging-in-Publication Data
Names: Mara, Wil, author.
Title: Be a plumber / by Wil Mara.
Description: Ann Arbor, Michigan : Cherry Lake Publishing, [2019] | Series: 21st century skills library | Includes bibliographical references and index.
Identifiers: LCCN 2019003498| ISBN 9781534148192 (lib. bdg.) | ISBN 9781534149625 (pdf) | ISBN 9781534151055 (pbk.) | ISBN 9781534152489 (ebook)
Subjects: LCSH: Plumbing—Vocational guidance—Juvenile literature.
Classification: LCC TH6130 .M37 2019 | DDC 696/.1023—dc23
LC record available at https://lccn.loc.gov/2019003498

Cherry Lake Publishing would like to acknowledge the work of The Partnership for 21st Century Learning. Please visit *www.p21.org* for more information.

Printed in the United States of America
Corporate Graphics

ABOUT THE AUTHOR

Wil Mara is the author of over 175 fiction and nonfiction books for children. He has written many titles for Cherry Lake Publishing, including the popular *Global Citizens: Modern Media* and *Citizen's Guide* series. More about his work can be found at www.wilmara.com.

TABLE OF CONTENTS

CHAPTER 1

The Plumbing Life

Master plumber Andy Evans is stirred from a deep sleep in the middle of the night. His cell phone is ringing. Andy is used to waking up at odd hours. He's been in the plumbing business for more than 20 years, and he learned long ago that it's anything but a nine-to-five job. Andy already knows who is calling because he has a separate ringtone for each of his clients. He also already knows what the call is about. There's a plumbing emergency somewhere.

Andy answers the call and hears that he needs to get to the Bartletts' house. A pipe burst in the basement, and the house is flooding fast. Andy had been there a few months back,

Over time, pipes can rust and become weak until they eventually burst open.

installing a new sink in the first-floor bathroom. He had to go into the basement while he was there, and he noticed that some of the pipes were very old. The house was built in the 1950s. A few of the pipes were part of the original construction. Andy recommended that they be replaced, but the Bartletts didn't want to spend the money at the time.

Andy quickly gets dressed and hurries out to his van. "Evans Plumbing Services" is printed on a big magnetic sign

Plumbers use a wide variety of tools and other supplies to complete jobs.

that's stuck to the side. Andy's tools and other equipment are already inside it. He owns his own business, but he also does **contract** work for larger companies. He likes owning the business because he can make most of the decisions himself. He can also set his own schedule for most jobs.

Ten minutes later, Andy is driving up the Bartletts' street. Every house is dark and quiet except for theirs. Andy pulls into the driveway and hurries out. Once inside, he discovers just what he thought he would—one of the old pipes exploded under all the pressure, and now there's water gushing out. The water is already several inches deep in the basement, and it's rising higher every minute.

Andy finds the main water line that comes in from the street and turns it off. He sets a portable pump in the flooded area and starts pumping the water out through one of the

21st Century Content

On average, there are about half a million plumbers working in the United States in any given year. The states that employ the most are listed here:

California—48,000
Texas—42,000
New York—27,000
Florida—24,000
Illinois—16,000

When repairing a burst pipe, a plumber needs to determine how much of the pipe needs to be replaced.

basement windows. It'll take a long time to get it all out. There will be a lot of damage to the walls, flooring, and anything else that was stored downstairs. Andy notices wet cardboard boxes with "Holiday decorations," "Winter clothes," and other descriptions written on them. The washer and dryer are sitting in the water. They might be damaged as well.

Once the water level starts to go down, Andy gets to work replacing the broken pipe. This will take a long time. The pipe is easy to see in some places but not in others. Parts of it run through the ceiling, and other parts go behind a small closet. But the whole thing will have to be fixed. The Bartletts are going to need a reliable flow of water into their home. How else will they take showers, wash their laundry, or run the dishwasher? They want to be able to do all these things without worrying about another plumbing emergency in the future.

Sloshing through the water in his rubber boots, Andy goes upstairs and back out to the van to get the equipment he needs. It's going to be a long night, but he is ready for it. To him, it's all part of the excitement of being a plumber.

CHAPTER 2

Becoming a Plumber

The road to a career in plumbing starts with education. An advanced college degree is not necessary, but there is still plenty to learn. Many of the topics taught in high school are of value to future plumbers. Math is very important. Everything from basic addition and subtraction all the way to algebra and geometry will be helpful to plumbers. Having some knowledge of science, especially physics, is also very useful.

Following high school, a future plumber can go straight into training under the guidance of other plumbers. But it is sometimes better to attend some type of vocational school

Basic math skills are essential knowledge for anyone who is thinking of becoming a plumber.

In vocational school, a plumber will learn how to
cut and bend pipes using special tools.

first. Such schools can be anything from trade and technical schools to community colleges that have specialized plumbing courses. There are also more online opportunities than ever before, and this is likely to continue growing in the future.

Most schools offer a two-year program. Aside from basic plumbing techniques, students learn how to use and care for different types of equipment. These include hand tools such as pipe wrenches, channel locks, hose cutters, and **augers**. They also include power tools such as hole saws, hacksaws, soldering irons, and **welding** torches. Students also learn about the latest plumbing technologies and related fields such as the installation and maintenance of heating and cooling systems. Some learning will take place in the classroom, but much of it will be hands-on. Students can also take courses in business, in case they wish to start their own company at some point. Graduation from a vocational school will result in some type of official certification.

The next step is to secure job experience through an **apprenticeship**. This is when a young plumber is taught the

Plumbers need to be able to understand blueprints and other documents relating to their work.

trade by a professional who has been on the job for many years. During an apprenticeship, the student earns a salary while developing skills working in real-life situations. The average apprenticeship lasts from four to five years. Apprentices learn about everything from proper tool usage and piping methods to **blueprint** reading, safety procedures, and local building codes.

Following an apprenticeship, a plumber will become a **journeyman**. This is the term for someone who has completed the apprenticeship program and is now certified to work without supervision. The only remaining level after journeyman is master plumber. In most cases, this

Life and Career Skills

There are many different careers within the larger field of plumbing. The most common job is that of a plumbing technician. This is the person who comes to your home to fix everyday issues such as leaks and clogs.

A pipe fitter installs and repairs piping that is usually used in larger facilities, such as businesses and factories.

Steamfitters specialize in pipe systems that are used for heating, ventilating, or refrigeration systems.

There are also pipe layers, who assure that underground piping is correctly designed and installed so it will last many years. These pipes transport everything from fresh drinking water to sewage and other waste.

Plumbers often find themselves working in tight spaces where there is little room to move.

certification is achieved following two to three years as a journeyman. A master plumber is qualified to not only perform all plumbing tasks but also oversee work **sites** and plan and design full plumbing systems. A journeyman will also need to pass several tests to reach master status. The exact content of the tests varies from state to state. Some tests are written, while others are practical. This means the plumber's skills will be tested in real situations.

CHAPTER 3

Pros and Cons

The plumbing trade, like any other profession, comes with both risks and rewards. For many plumbers, one of the most satisfying aspects of the job is fixing people's problems. The average person has no idea how to fix a plumbing issue. And even if they did, they likely wouldn't have the tools or the skills to do the job.

Many plumbers also like that they are not stuck in an office at a desk job. They are usually on the road going from one job site to another, so they are never in the same place. There is also plenty of variety in the work itself. Plumbing is not just

Working in a variety of environments is one of the best parts of being a plumber. Here, a pipe fitter installs a heating system in a building.

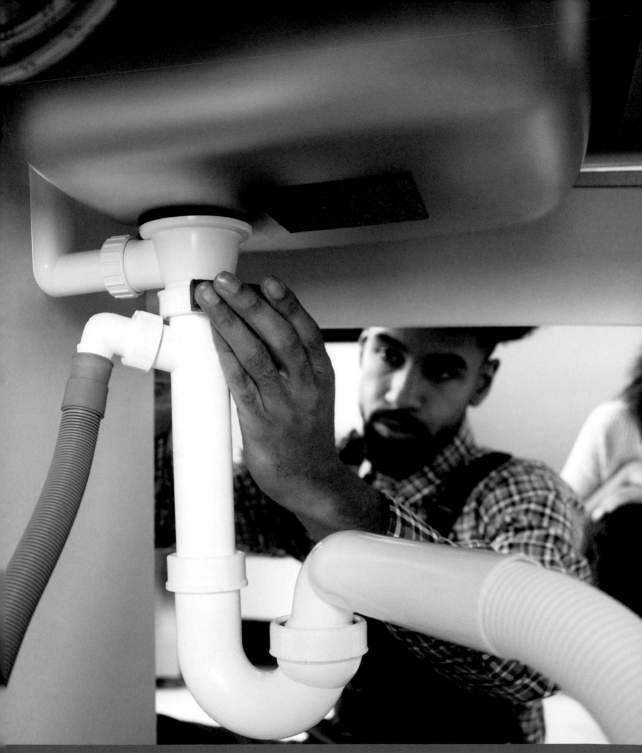

Many plumbers focus on everyday household
repairs, such as fixing leaky sinks.

simply fixing leaky faucets or replacing worn-out toilet **gaskets**. In an ordinary home, a plumber will be faced with any number of problems, including reduced water pressure, clogged drains, and **sump pump** failures. Sinks, toilets, bathtubs, water heaters, or other appliances sometimes need to be replaced. Each day is a new adventure, as well as an opportunity to continue learning through experience. Even master plumbers cannot honestly say they've seen it all!

Pay varies a lot from one plumbing job to another. One of the main factors is experience. For example, a master plumber who has been on the job for 30 years usually makes more money than an apprentice. Location is also important. Areas with higher populations have the greatest plumbing needs, so wages tend to be higher.

Plumbers can improve their pay and benefits by joining a **union**. Union leaders negotiate for higher pay and other important benefits, such as a retirement fund or health insurance. In some situations, a plumber will have the opportunity to work overtime. Overtime pay is typically

Plumbers might work alone or together with a small team, depending on the type of work that needs to be done.

higher than pay earned during normal hours. However, overtime work often requires sacrificing weeknights, weekends, or holidays.

The risks of being a plumber might not be as high as being a professional stuntperson, but the chance of injury is still greater than in many other jobs. Plumbers need to be careful to avoid getting cuts from sharp tools or from the ends of cut pieces of metal. They also watch out for hot pipes and the equipment used for soldering and welding. They don't want to get burned. Anyone interested in the plumbing profession should take the time to become familiar with all safety procedures.

Plumbers crawl into tight spaces, and sometimes they work outside in bad weather conditions. They also need to do a certain amount of heavy lifting. This means they will need to be in good physical shape.

21st Century Content

Roughly two-thirds of all plumbers in the United States are contractors. About 13 percent are self-employed. The rest of them work for the government or in factories. Statistics show that plumbing is one of the fastest-growing professions in the country, with an annual increase of around 16 percent. This growth is likely due to the currently strong economy, which usually stirs home improvement spending as well as new home construction. The national average salary for a plumber is around $53,000 per year.

CHAPTER 4

Rules and Regulations

It is not enough for plumbers to complete schooling and an apprenticeship before they can work legally. Anyone looking to become a professional plumber also needs to be **licensed**.

The first step of getting a license is to contact the state's licensing board to see what is required. Some requirements are very basic, such as age (18 is the usual minimum), a clean police record, and the ability to communicate in English.

The licensing process usually involves both written and practical testing to assure that a person's skills are at a certain level. When plumbers arrive for testing, they are usually required to bring a photo ID, Social Security card, diplomas and other proof of education, and a licensing application.

A burst water pipe inside a wall can cause a lot of damage to the surrounding area.

A small fee may be involved. Some states conduct a background investigation to dig deeper into the person's history. A few states offer courses that help prepare for the licensing test. Much of this can be done online. If a plumber fails the licensing test, it can often be taken again at a later date.

Just as important as getting licensed is getting **bonded**. Being bonded means a plumber is insured if he or she causes damage to someone's property while on the job. Although every plumber tries to avoid causing problems, accidents

Dealing with customers is an important part of
the job for plumbers who do house calls.

Life and Career Skills

If you're thinking about running your own plumbing company one day, you would do well to study some basic aspects of business. These include project management, cost estimation, and customer relations.

Project management is an important skill for anyone who is running a business. This means being able to keep track of which projects need to get done and which tasks different employees are working on. It also means being able to make important decisions, answer questions, and accept responsibility when things go wrong.

Cost estimation is the practice of looking at a potential job and figuring out how much to charge. A plumber needs to determine how much it will cost to buy necessary supplies and how long it will take to fix the problem before the job even gets started. This way, they can give the client an accurate estimate of how much the job will cost.

Customer relations is important in any business. Keeping clients happy will encourage them to recommend you to their friends. On the other hand, if they are unhappy with your work, they could fire you and have someone else complete the job. They might even post a negative review of your business online.

Building codes contain specific rules for installing sinks and other appliances.

happen. The odds are good that it will happen at least once over the course of a plumber's career. For example, a plumber who accidentally causes a pipe to burst would be responsible for any resulting damage. If the damage is severe, the plumber might not be able to afford to pay for it. But a bond prevents the plumber from having to worry about this. When an accident occurs, the bond company pays for any damages.

There are several requirements for becoming bonded. First, a plumber must be licensed. This tells the bond company that the plumber has a certain level of knowledge and experience. The plumber also should have a work history clear of previous incidents. A plumber who has caused damage in the past may still be able to get bonded. But it becomes more difficult and more expensive. Any plumber who is unbonded will have a tough time finding work. After all, people usually don't want to take a chance on someone they don't feel they can trust.

Plumbers have to follow rules while they are on the job. Pipes and appliances can't just be installed any which way. They have to observe local building codes. Building codes are rules that determine how different structures should be built in different situations. They vary from city to city and state to state. They are put in place for safety and to ensure that buildings work correctly. For example, codes might require that pipes be made from a certain material in order to keep the water clean and drinkable. Or they might require that a shower be hooked up to a drainage system in a specific way.

These rules and regulations might sound like a lot to keep track of. But it is just part of the job for a plumber. With hard work and experience, it all becomes second nature.

Think About It

As long as humans have tried to channel water in one direction or another, workers have been needed to fix plumbing problems. Some of the earliest known plumbing efforts were constructed around 3500 BCE, when pipes were used to redirect the waters of the Indus River in India. What purpose do you think this early plumbing system served? And what kind of problems do you think there were back then that aren't as much of a concern today?

There's plenty of information online about different types of plumbing careers. Which one do you feel would be right for you, and why? What aspects of the plumbing profession do you think you'd like the most and the least?

Find Out More

BOOK

Gregory, Josh. *Plumber*. Ann Arbor, MI: Cherry Lake Publishing, 2011.

WEBSITES

Best Way to Become a Plumber
www.benjaminfranklinplumbingiowa.com/how-to-become-a-plumber
Find out what it takes to enter the plumbing profession, step-by-step.

Plumbing Tips for Kids and Teens
www.wislerplumbing.com/plumbing-tips-for-kidsteens
Learn some household plumbing basics with these tips for kids.

U.S. Bureau of Labor Statistics—Occupational Outlook Handbook: Plumbers, Pipefitters, and Steamfitters
www.bls.gov/ooh/construction-and-extraction/plumbers-pipefitters-and-steamfitters.htm
Learn how to become a plumber, how the profession is expected to grow, and more at this government site.

GLOSSARY

apprenticeship (uh-PREN-tis-ship) training situation in which someone learns a skill by working with an expert on the job

augers (AW-gurz) snakelike tools designed to run through pipes and other water lines to break up clogs and other blockage

blueprint (BLOO-print) a drawing that illustrates how a structure needs to be built

bonded (BAHND-id) protected by an insurance policy that covers damages caused by a worker while on the job

contract (KAHN-trakt) a written business agreement between two or more parties

gaskets (GAS-kits) rubber rings that create a seal between pipes or other objects

journeyman (JUR-nee-man) a plumber who has more experience, knowledge, and

skill than an apprentice, but not as much as a master

licensed (LYE-suhnsd) officially certified to perform a job

master (MAS-tur) the highest recognized level of a professional plumber in terms of experience, knowledge, and skill

sites (SITES) locations of plumbing jobs

sump pump (SUHMP PUHMP) a pump designed to remove water from one location and transfer it to another

union (YOON-yuhn) an organization that protects the interests of a certain type of worker, such as a plumber

welding (WEL-ding) the process of connecting two or more pieces of metal through extreme heating and the application of a bonding agent

INDEX